ANIMAL CONTROL
OFFICER

BY CHRIS BOWMAN

BELLWETHER MEDIA · MINNEAPOLIS, MN

Are you ready to take it to the extreme?
Torque books thrust you into the action-packed world
of sports, vehicles, mystery, and adventure. These books
may include dirt, smoke, fire, and dangerous stunts.
WARNING: read at your own risk.

Library of Congress Cataloging-in-Publication Data

Bowman, Chris, 1990- author.
  Animal Control Officer / by Chris Bowman.
      pages cm. -- (Torque: Dangerous Jobs)
  Summary: "Engaging images accompany information about animal control officers. The combination
of high-interest subject matter and light text is intended for students in grades 3 through 7"-- Provided by
publisher.
  Audience: Ages 7-12.
  Audience: Grades 3 to 7.
  Includes bibliographical references and index.
  ISBN 978-1-62617-109-1 (hardcover : alk. paper)
1. Animal welfare--Juvenile literature. 2. Dangerous animals--Control--Juvenile literature. I. Title. II.
Series: Dangerous jobs (Minneapolis, Minn.)
  HV4708.B686 2014
  636.08'32--dc23

                                    2013050080

This edition first published in 2015 by Bellwether Media, Inc.

Printed in the United States of America, North Mankato, MN.

TABLE OF CONTENTS

CHAPTER 1

DOG ATTACK!

A man is out running in his neighborhood. He sees a big stray dog in the street ahead. Suddenly, the dog starts barking and charges at him. The man backs away, but the dog still tries to bite him. The man barely escapes to a neighbor's house.

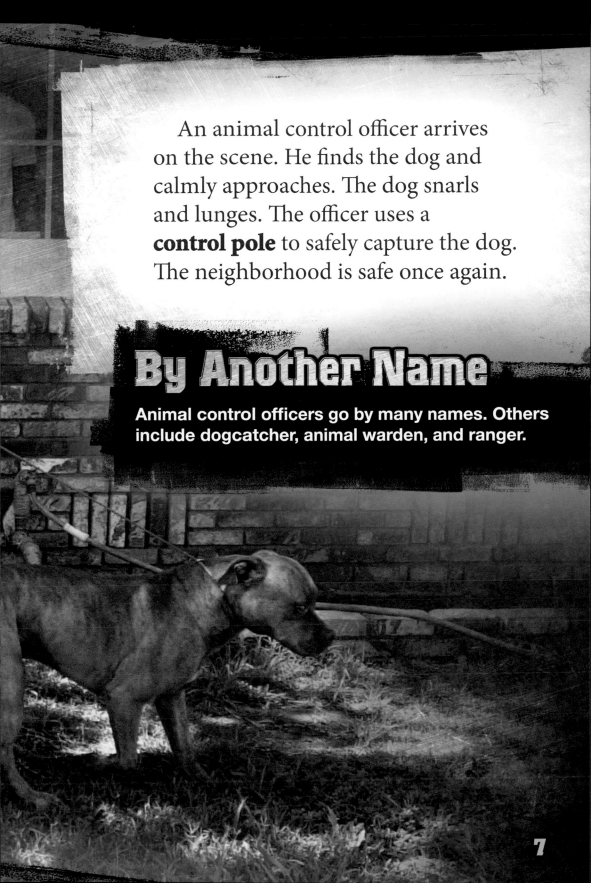

An animal control officer arrives on the scene. He finds the dog and calmly approaches. The dog snarls and lunges. The officer uses a **control pole** to safely capture the dog. The neighborhood is safe once again.

By Another Name

Animal control officers go by many names. Others include dogcatcher, animal warden, and ranger.

CHAPTER 2

ANIMAL CONTROL OFFICERS

Animal control officers work for cities or counties. Their job is to make sure laws involving pets and wild animals are followed. They work in health, police, or park departments of local governments. Officers answer emergency calls and capture stray animals. Sometimes they explore cases of animal **cruelty**. They also teach communities about being responsible pet owners.

Handle With Care

Animal control officers also check on pet shops and animal shelters. They make sure the animals are treated well.

Requirements to become an animal control officer vary by area. Some officers study **criminal justice** or **animal science** in college. Most officers have experience training or caring for animals. Almost all animal control officers are trained by other officers on the job. They also learn all important laws that involve animals.

Safety is at the heart of everything animal control officers do. They must be careful when handling dangerous animals. Animal control officers are trained in **first aid** to help **victims** of animal attacks. Most officers can give animals first aid, too. They try to protect the animal, especially in animal rescues.

Animal control officers have many tools to safely handle animals. They wear gloves to protect their hands from bites and scratches. Officers use **cat grabbers** and control poles to rescue animals from hard-to-reach places. Long hooks and **baggers** are used on loose snakes. Officers use **bite sticks** and **live traps** on other dangerous animals. Sometimes they must use **tranquilizer guns**.

A rescued animal is returned to its owner or taken to a clinic or animal shelter. Wild animals are often released back into nature.

CHAPTER 3

DANGER!

Animal control officers face a wide variety of animals and situations. This includes handling wild animals. These animals are more likely to attack people. Sometimes they have diseases like **rabies** that make them **aggressive**. Pets usually attack only if they have been mistreated and do not trust people.

Wild animals are not the only danger to officers. The stress of dealing with suffering animals can lead to accidents or injury. Some animal owners become angry when their pet is being captured. These people can become a danger to themselves and the officers.

Animal control officers know that handling animals can be dangerous. However, they like working with animals. Their brave work saves many people from animal attacks. They also protect many animals from cruel treatment and harm.

Tragedy on the Job

On September 29, 2009, Animal Control Officer Theresa Foss was fatally injured in Plainfield, Connecticut. Officer Foss was answering a call about an aggressive dog that had scared a family. On the call, Officer Foss was knocked to the ground. She suffered head injuries and died soon after the accident.

Glossary

aggressive—ready to attack

animal science—the study of raising and caring for pets and livestock

baggers—long bags with a tube at the bottom; baggers are used to control snakes.

bite sticks—long sticks used during dog attacks; dogs bite the sticks, keeping the officers safe.

cat grabbers—long sticks that can grab cats and other small animals

control pole—a pole with a loop of cord on one end; control poles help officers reach animals.

criminal justice—government practices that deal with crime and criminals

cruelty—actions that cause suffering

first aid—emergency medical care given to a sick or injured person before he or she reaches a hospital; animal control officers also give first aid to animals.

live traps—metal cages used to capture animals without injuring or killing them

rabies—a deadly disease passed to people through animal bites

tranquilizer guns—guns that shoot darts to make animals rest; tranquilizer guns help officers safely handle wild or aggressive animals.

victims—people who are hurt, killed, or made to suffer

To Learn More

AT THE LIBRARY

Bowman, Chris. *Police Officer*. Minneapolis, Minn.: Bellwether Media, 2015.

Goldish, Meish. *Animal Control Officers to the Rescue*. New York, N.Y.: Bearport Pub., 2013.

Owings, Lisa. *Bear Attack*. Minneapolis, Minn.: Bellwether Media, 2013.

ON THE WEB

Learning more about animal control officers is as easy as 1, 2, 3.

1. Go to www.factsurfer.com.

2. Enter "animal control officers" into the search box.

3. Click the "Surf" button and you will see a list of related web sites.

With factsurfer.com, finding more information is just a click away.

Index